PreScripts

CURSIVE LETTERS AND COLORING

World History

PreScripts Cursive Letters and Coloring:
World History

Created by Courtney Sanford and Kelly Steigerwald
Layout by Kelly Steigerwald

Published in the U.S.A. by Classical Conversations, Inc.
P.O. Box 909
West End, NC 27376

ISBN: 978-0-9851701-5-8

For ordering information, visit www.ClassicalConversationsBooks.com.
Printed in the United States of America

PreScripts Cursive Letters and Coloring: World History

Why Learn Cursive?

Cursive writing is faster than printing, which can help students take notes in class quickly and get their ideas onto paper more easily. Students who write in cursive are less likely to have trouble reversing letters such as *b* and *d*. Furthermore, students who learn to read cursive can read handwritten documents, which opens up a world of history to them. They can read family letters and historical documents such as the Declaration of Independence.

Why Color?

In addition to being fun, coloring improves fine motor skills and hand–eye coordination. Coloring also helps children strengthen the muscles used in writing, making writing easier.

Why History?

Coloring these interesting images from history might spark interest in history, people, and cultures around the world. If your child is interested in learning more about the events and people he or she colors, you can read more about them at the library or from *Classical Acts & Facts History Cards*, available from ClassicalConversationsBooks.com.

What's Next?

For the next step in learning cursive and developing fine motor skills, progress to PreScripts Cursive Words and Drawing books available from ClassicalConversationsBooks.com.

Trace with your finger.

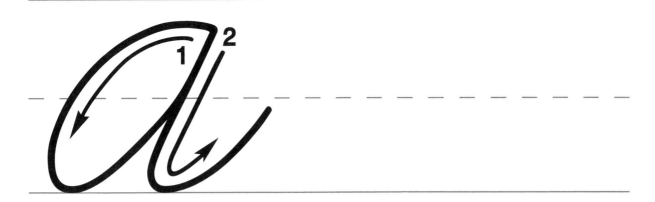

Trace with your pencil, then write.

Fowling in the Marshes

Egyptians

Trace with your finger.

Trace with your pencil, then write.

a a a a

a a a a

a a a a

MINOAN BULL-LEAPER

Trace with your finger.

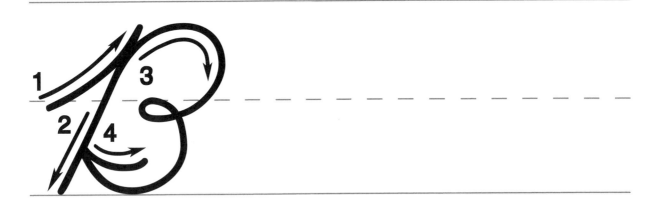

Trace with your pencil, then write.

GREAT PYRAMID AND SPHINX OF GIZA

SEVEN WONDERS OF THE ANCIENT WORLD

Trace with your finger.

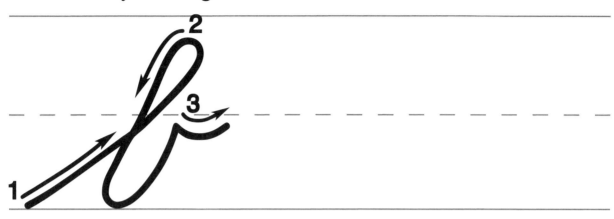

Trace with your pencil, then write.

HANGING GARDENS OF BABYLON

SEVEN WONDERS OF THE ANCIENT WORLD

Trace with your finger.

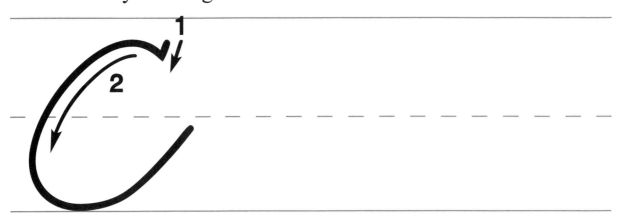

Trace with your pencil, then write.

TEMPLE OF ARTEMIS AT JERASH, JORDAN

SEVEN WONDERS OF THE ANCIENT WORLD

Trace with your finger.

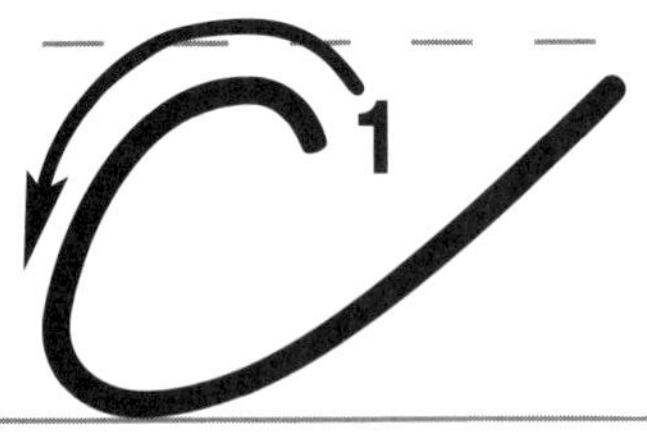

C

Trace with your pencil, then write.

C   C   C   C

C   C   C   C

C   C   C   C

STATUE OF ZEUS

SEVEN WONDERS OF THE ANCIENT WORLD

Trace with your finger.

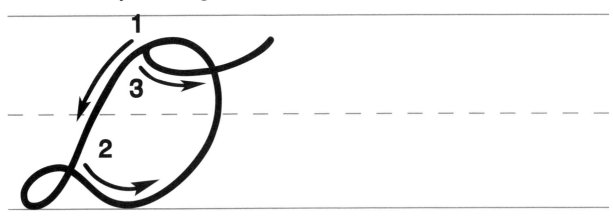

Trace with your pencil, then write.

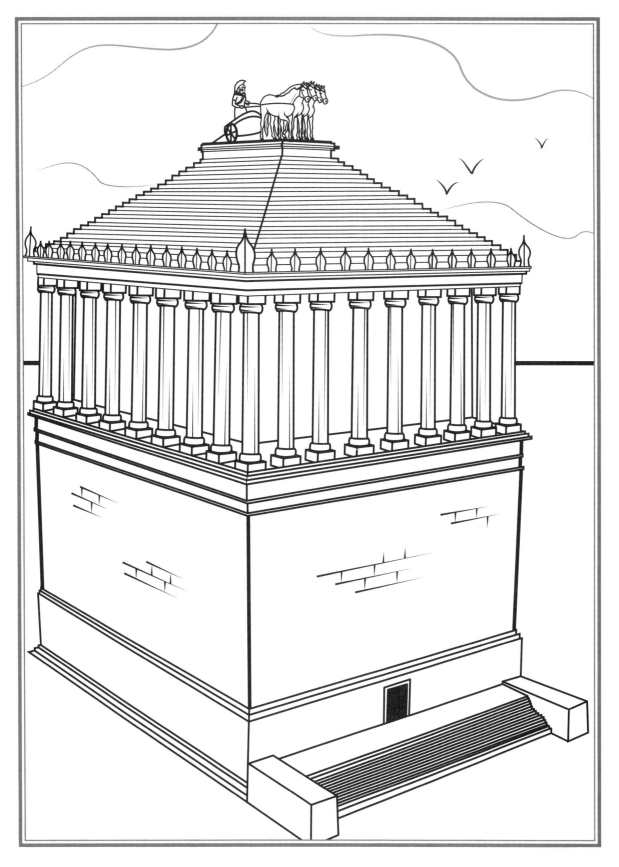

THE MAUSOLEUM AT HALICARNASSUS

SEVEN WONDERS OF THE ANCIENT WORLD

Trace with your finger.

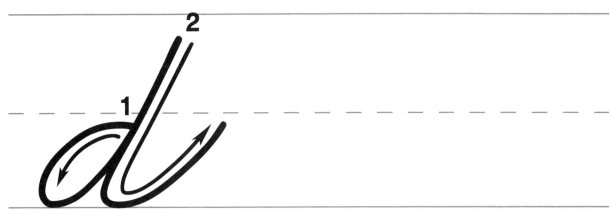

Trace with your pencil, then write.

Pharos Lighthouse

Seven Wonders of the Ancient World

Trace with your finger.

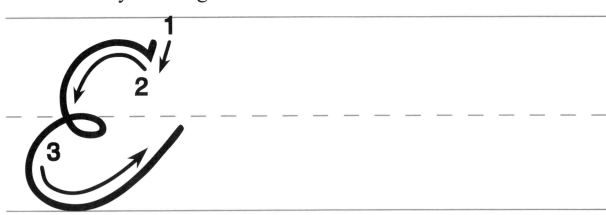

Trace with your pencil, then write.

COLOSSUS OF RHODES

SEVEN WONDERS OF THE ANCIENT WORLD

Trace with your finger.

2

1

Trace with your pencil, then write.

ℓ   ℓ   ℓ   ℓ

ℓ   ℓ   ℓ   ℓ

ℓ   ℓ   ℓ   ℓ

PYRAMIDS OF MEROË

KUSH

Trace with your finger.

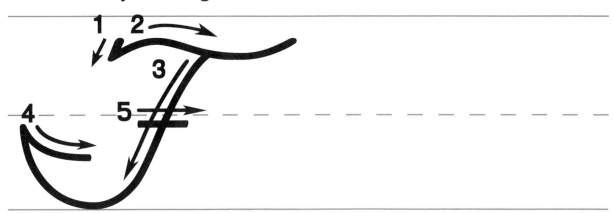

Trace with your pencil, then write.

CLASSICALCONVERSATIONS.COM

KING T'ANG OF CHINA'S SHANG DYNASTY

Trace with your finger.

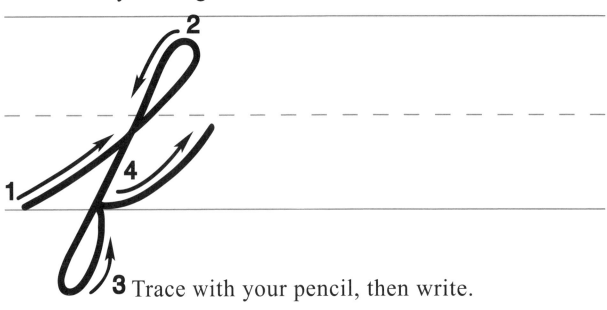

3 Trace with your pencil, then write.

f   *f*   *f*   *f*

f   *f*   *f*   *f*

f   *f*   *f*   *f*

OLMEC COLOSSAL HEAD STATUE

OLMECS OF MESOAMERICA

Trace with your finger.

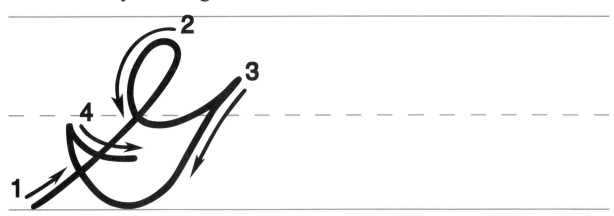

Trace with your pencil, then write.

ROMULUS AND REMUS

ROME FOUNDED

Trace with your finger.

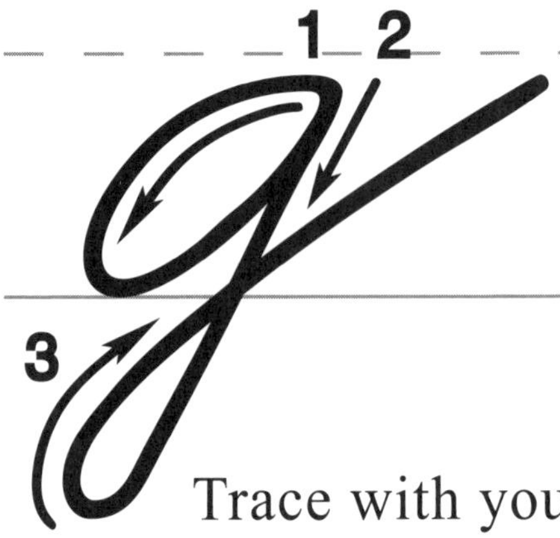

g

1 **2**

3

Trace with your pencil, then write.

g   g   g   g

g   g   g   g

g   g   g   g

THE ATTACK OF TIGLATH-PILESER III

ASSYRIAN EMPIRE

Trace with your finger.

Trace with your pencil, then write.

CONFUCIUS AND BUDDHA

Trace with your finger.

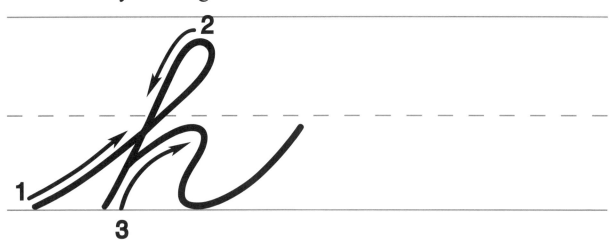

Trace with your pencil, then write.

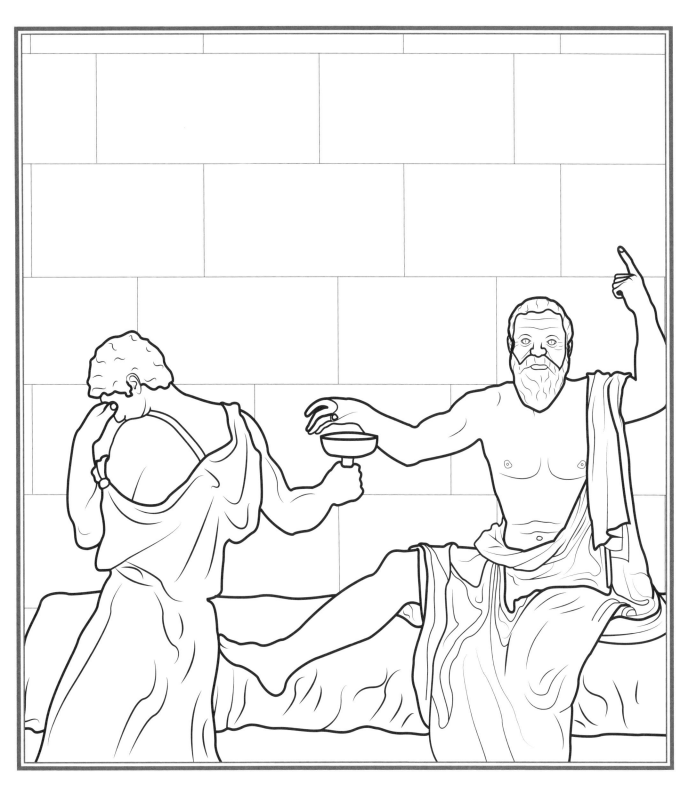

THE DEATH OF SOCRATES

THE GOLDEN AGE OF GREECE

Trace with your finger.

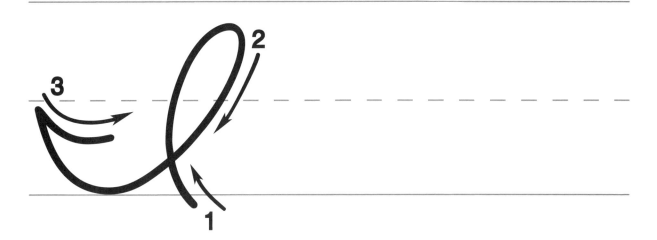

Trace with your pencil, then write.

MAYAN PYRAMID

MESOAMERICA

Trace with your finger.

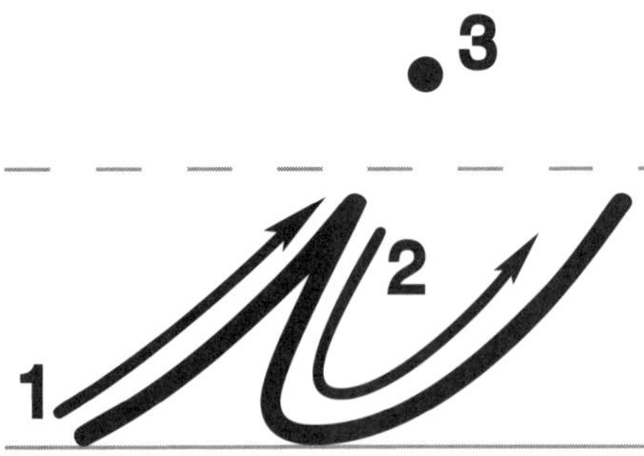

Trace with your pencil, then write.

i i i i

i i i i

i i i i

HANNIBAL CROSSING THE ALPS

PUNIC WARS

Trace with your finger.

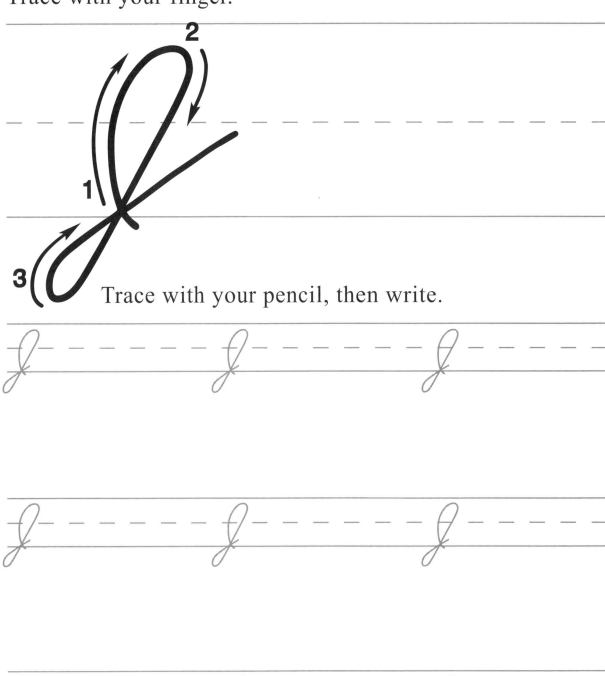

Trace with your pencil, then write.

JESUS THE MESSIAH

Trace with your finger.

Trace with your pencil, then write.

BYZANTINE EMPEROR JUSTINIAN

Trace with your finger.

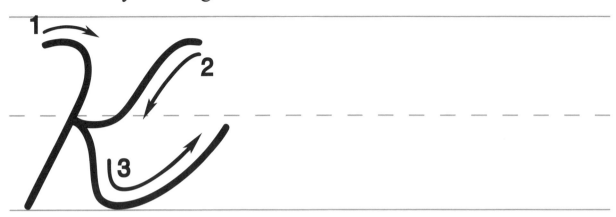

Trace with your pencil, then write.

ZANJ AND EARLY GHANA IN AFRICA

Trace with your finger.

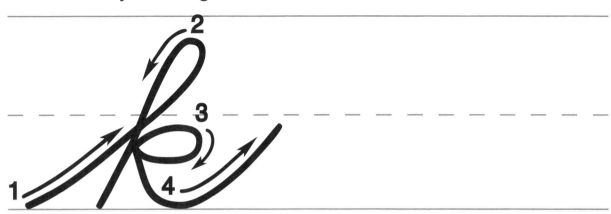

Trace with your pencil, then write.

THE FLYING CARPET

GOLDEN AGE OF ISLAM

Trace with your finger.

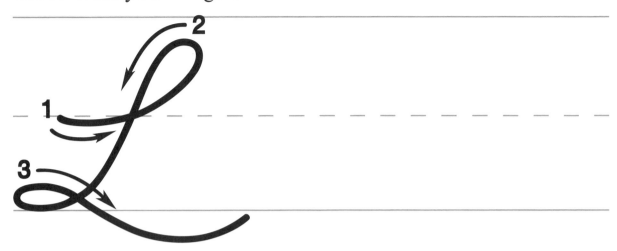

Trace with your pencil, then write.

 CLASSICALCONVERSATIONS.COM

VIKINGS RAID AND TRADE

Trace with your finger.

Trace with your pencil, then write.

CHARLEMAGNE CROWNED EMPEROR OF EUROPE

Trace with your finger.

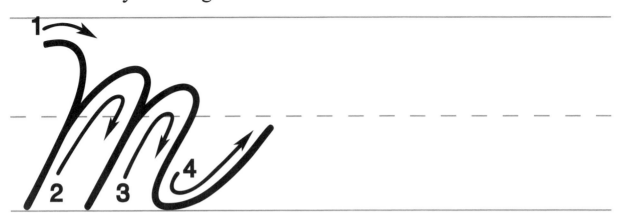

Trace with your pencil, then write.

BYZANTINE EMPEROR BASIL II

Trace with your finger.

Trace with your pencil, then write.

m m m

m m m

m m m

BASILICA ROOF IN FLORENCE, ITALY

EAST-WEST SCHISM OF THE CHURCH

Trace with your finger.

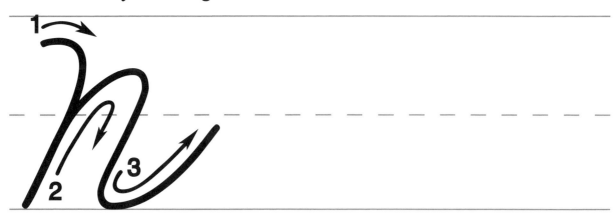

Trace with your pencil, then write.

EASTERN-ORTHODOX CUPOLA IN RUSSIA

EAST-WEST SCHISM OF THE CHURCH

Trace with your finger.

m

1 2

Trace with your pencil, then write.

m   m   m   m

m   m   m   m

m   m   m   m

THE NÁNDORFEHÉRVÁR BATTLE

THE CRUSADES

Trace with your finger.

Trace with your pencil, then write.

JAPAN'S SHOGUNS

Trace with your finger.

Trace with your pencil, then write.

King John Signs the Magna Carta

Trace with your finger.

Trace with your pencil, then write.

JOAN OF ARC

THE HUNDRED YEARS' WAR

Trace with your finger.

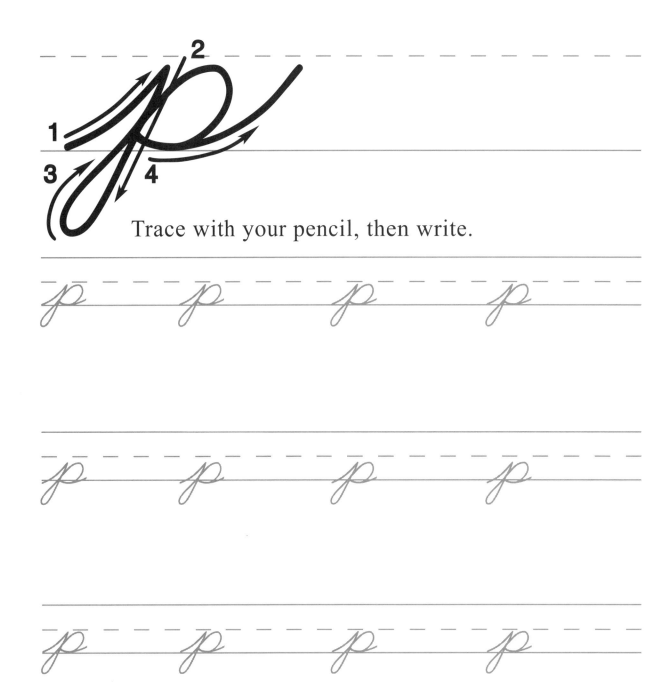

Trace with your pencil, then write.

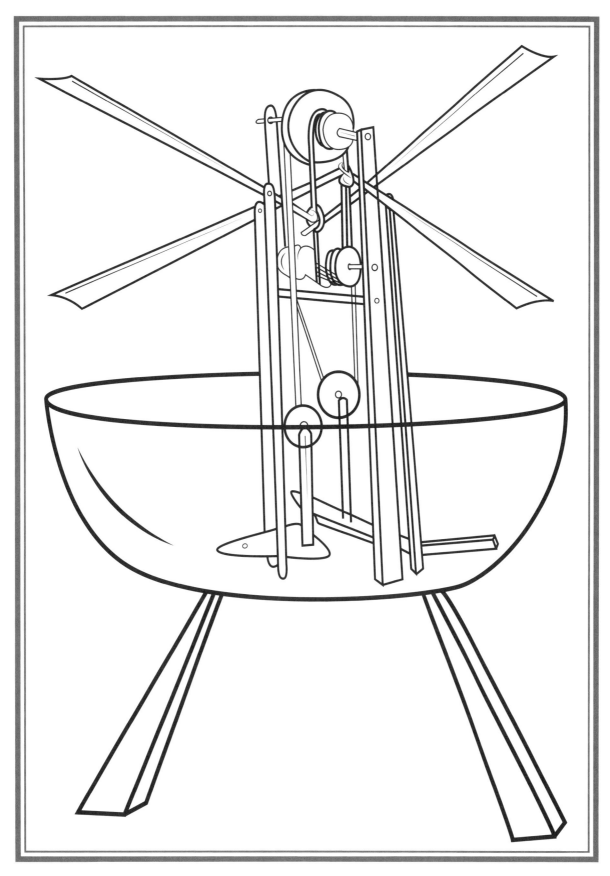

LEONARDO DA VINCI'S FLYING MACHINE

THE RENAISSANCE

Trace with your finger.

Trace with your pencil, then write.

AGE OF EXPLORATION

Trace with your finger.

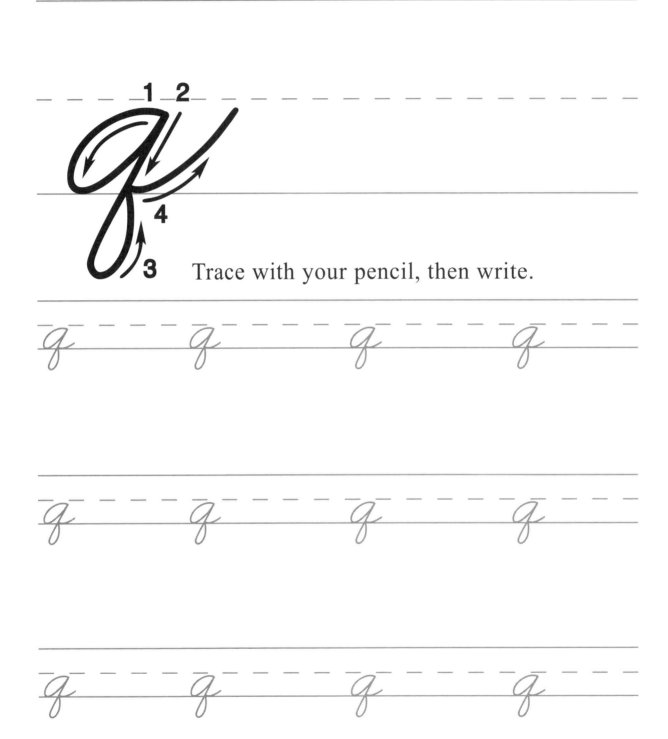

Trace with your pencil, then write.

q q q q

q q q q

q q q q

CZAR IVAN THE GREAT OF RUSSIA

Trace with your finger.

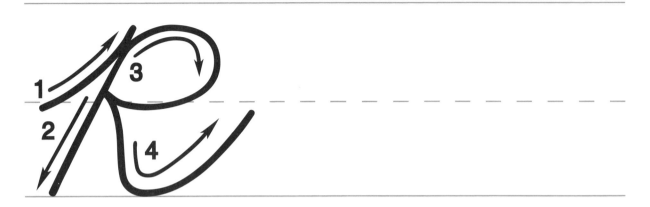

Trace with your pencil, then write.

COLUMBUS SAILS TO THE CARIBBEAN

Trace with your finger.

Trace with your pencil, then write.

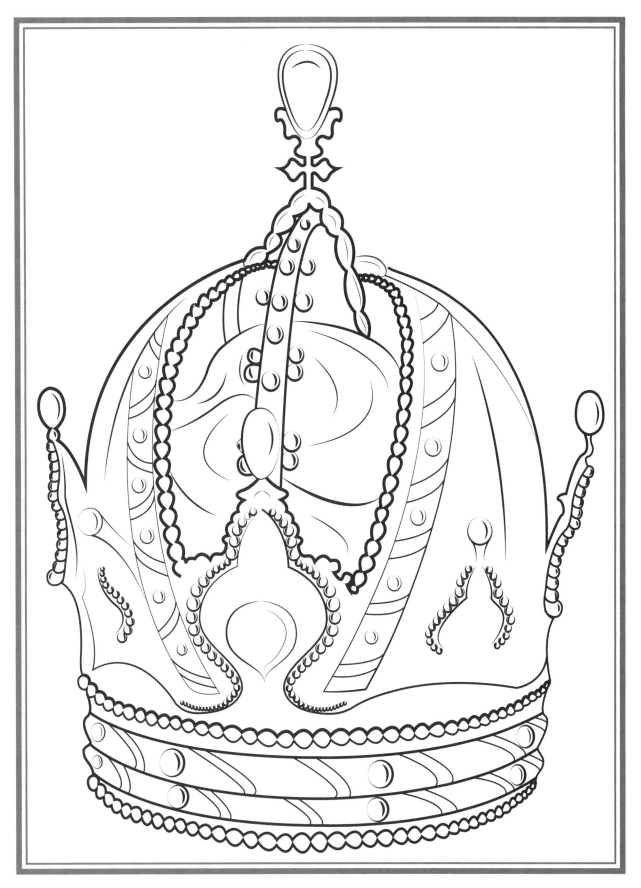

AGE OF ABSOLUTE MONARCHS

Trace with your finger.

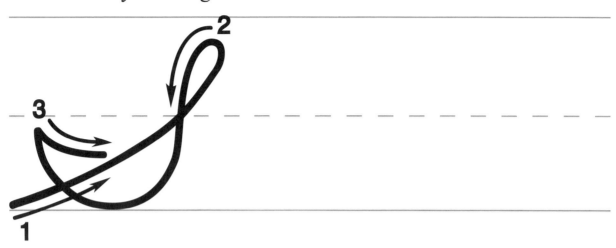

Trace with your pencil, then write.

NEW TESTAMENT TRANSLATION BY MARTIN LUTHER

PROTESTANT REFORMATION

Trace with your finger.

Trace with your pencil, then write.

SPANISH CONQUISTADORS IN THE AMERICAS

Trace with your finger.

Trace with your pencil, then write.

CLASSICAL CONVERSATIONS . COM

JAMESTOWN FOUNDED

Trace with your finger.

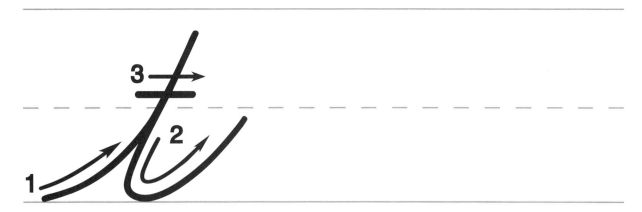

Trace with your pencil, then write.

DAVIS VERTICAL SEWING MACHINE

AGE OF INDUSTRY

Trace with your finger.

Trace with your pencil, then write.

AMERICAN REVOLUTION AND GENERAL GEORGE WASHINGTON

Trace with your finger.

Trace with your pencil, then write.

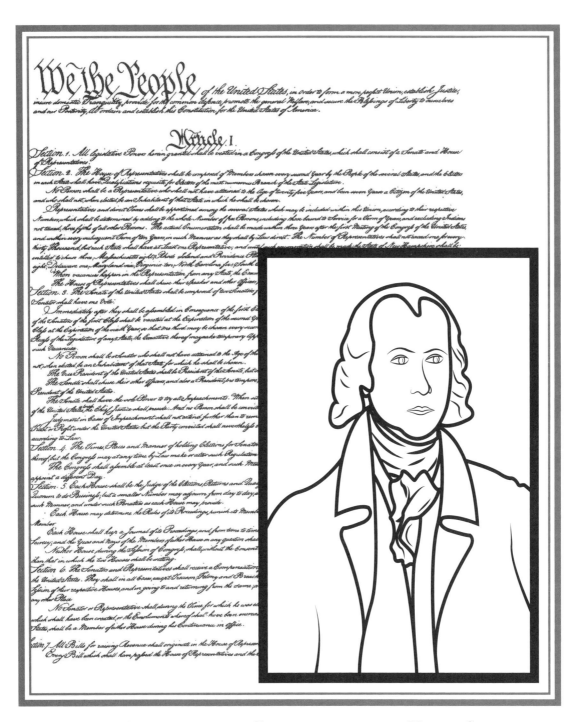

JAMES MADISON AND THE CONSTITUTION OF THE UNITED STATES

Trace with your finger.

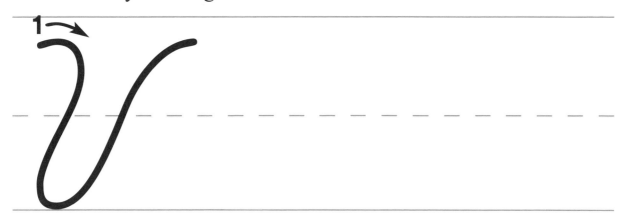

Trace with your pencil, then write.

CLASSICAL CONVERSATIONS . COM

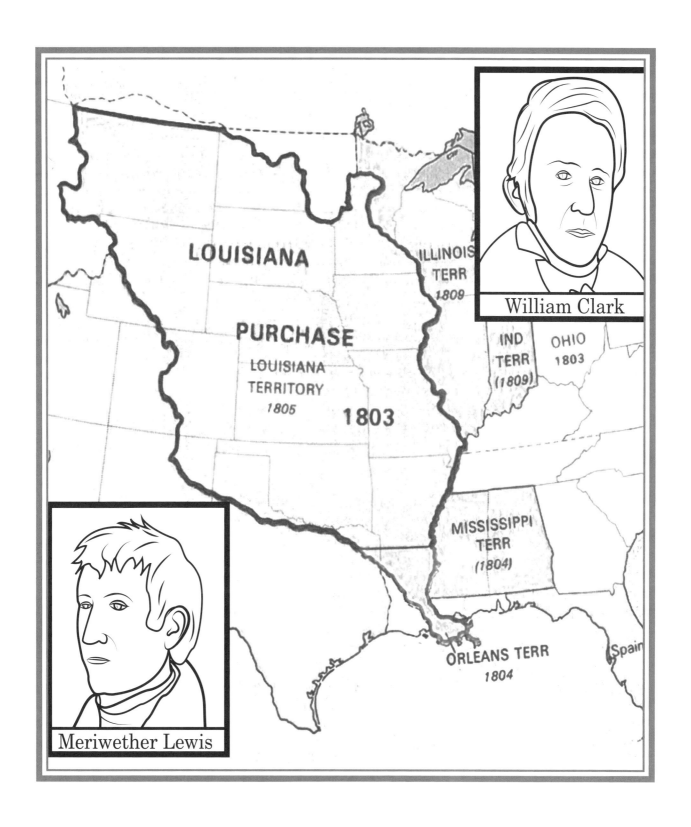

LOUISIANA PURCHASE AND THE LEWIS AND CLARK EXPEDITION

Trace with your finger.

Trace with your pencil, then write.

NAPOLEON CROWNED EMPEROR OF FRANCE

Trace with your finger.

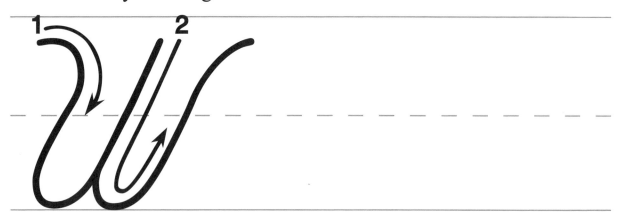

Trace with your pencil, then write.

THE WAR OF 1812

Trace with your finger.

Trace with your pencil, then write.

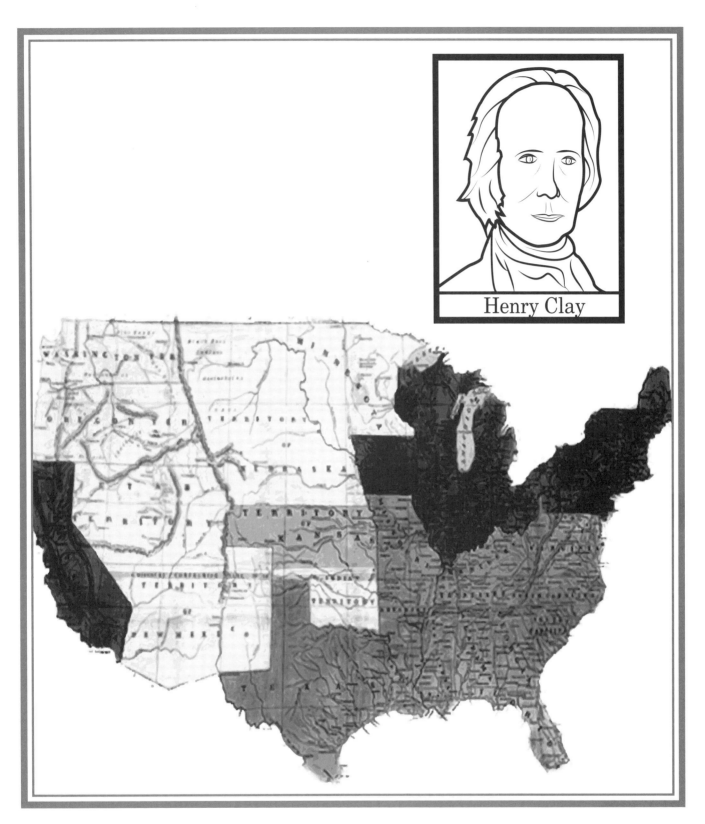

THE MISSOURI COMPROMISE AND HENRY CLAY

Trace with your finger.

Trace with your pencil, then write.

STATUE OF LIBERTY WELCOMES IMMIGRANTS TO AMERICA

Trace with your finger.

Trace with your pencil, then write.

THE MONROE DOCTRINE

Trace with your finger.

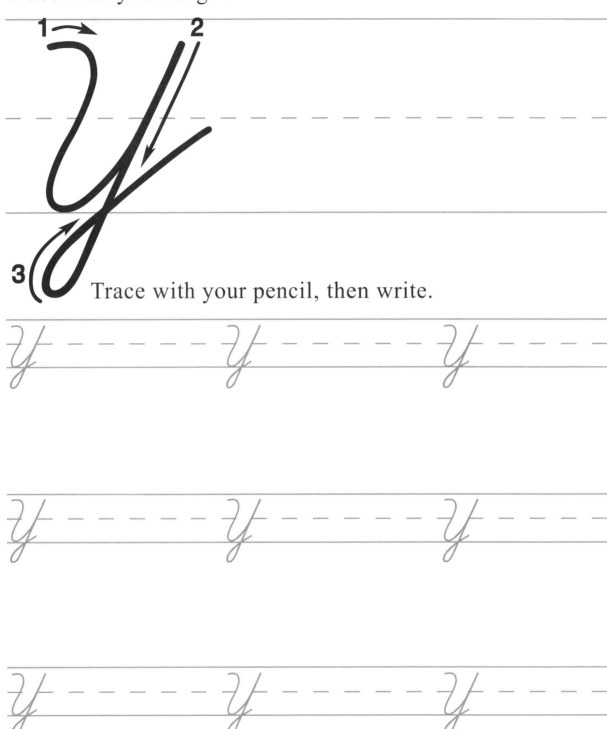

Trace with your pencil, then write.

CHEROKEE TRAIL OF TEARS

Trace with your finger.

Trace with your pencil, then write.

CALIFORNIA GOLD RUSH

U.S. WESTWARD EXPANSION

Trace with your finger.

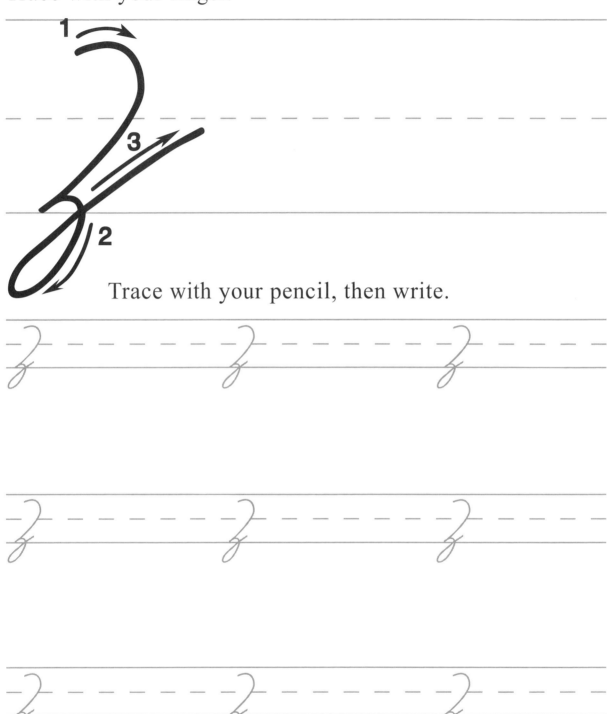

Trace with your pencil, then write.

THE COMPROMISE OF 1850

Trace with your finger.

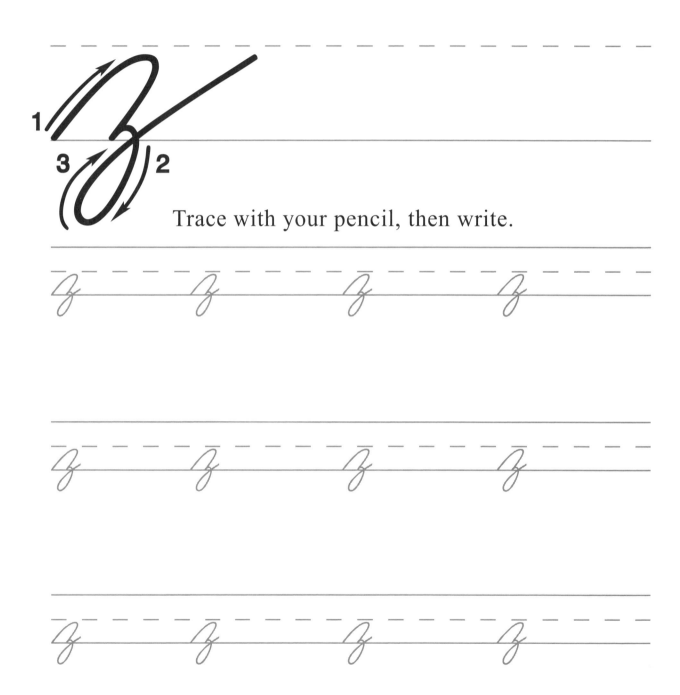

Trace with your pencil, then write.

STEAM LOCOMOTIVE

AGE OF INDUSTRY

Trace with your finger.

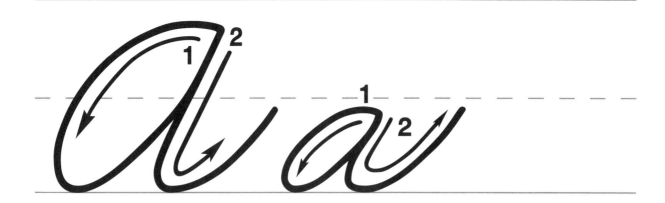

Trace with your pencil, then write.

C L A S S I C A L C O N V E R S A T I O N S . C O M

PRESIDENT LINCOLN AND THE WAR BETWEEN THE STATES

Trace with your finger.

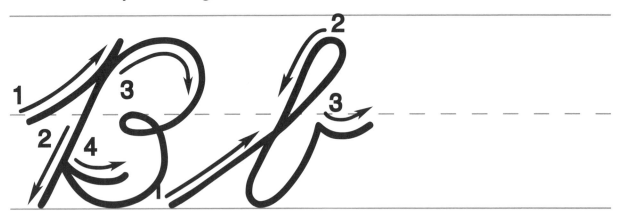

Trace with your pencil, then write.

ULYSSES S. GRANT: GENERAL OF THE UNION ARMY AND U.S. PRESIDENT

Trace with your finger.

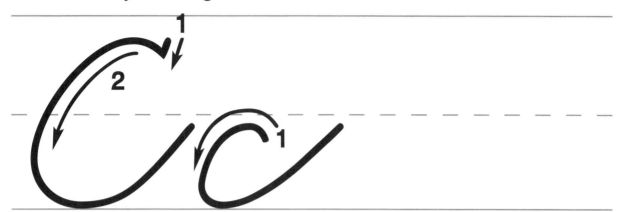

Trace with your pencil, then write.

THE CHARGE OF THE ROUGH RIDERS

THE SPANISH-AMERICAN WAR

Trace with your finger.

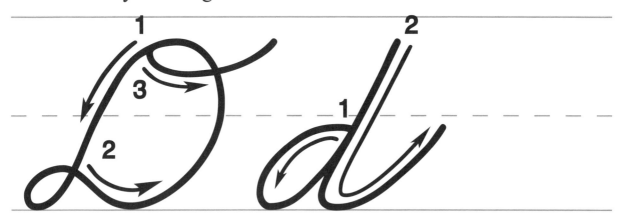

Trace with your pencil, then write.

CLASSICALCONVERSATIONS.COM

WORLD WAR I

Trace with your finger.

Trace with your pencil, then write.

STARRY NIGHT BY VINCENT VAN GOGH

MODERN PERIOD OF THE ARTS

Trace with your finger.

Trace with your pencil, then write.

THE GREAT DEPRESSION

Trace with your finger.

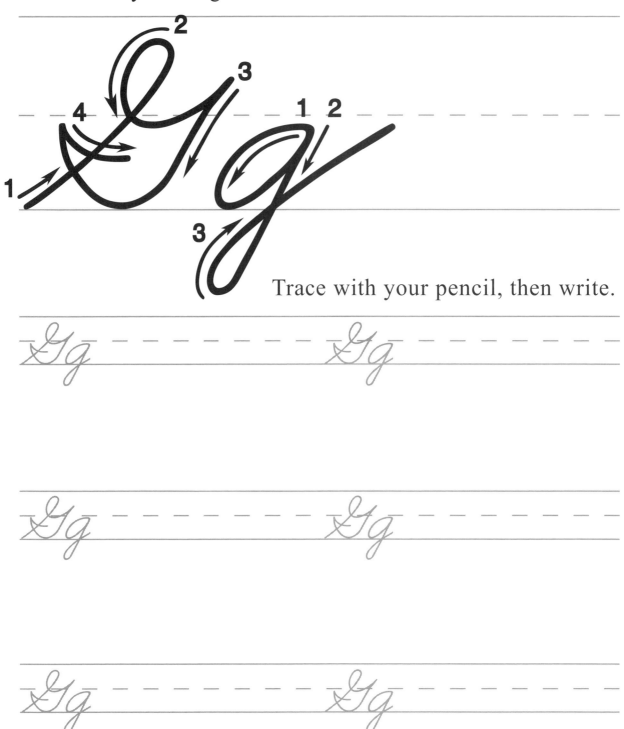

Trace with your pencil, then write.

WORLD WAR II

Trace with your finger.

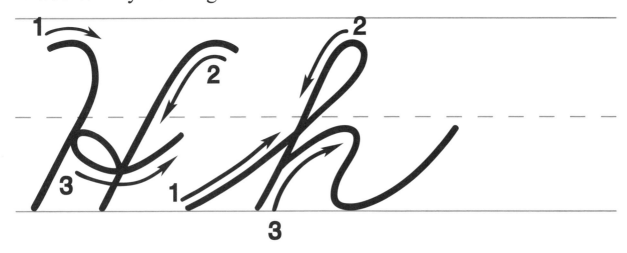

Trace with your pencil, then write.

STALIN OF THE U.S.S.R.

Trace with your finger.

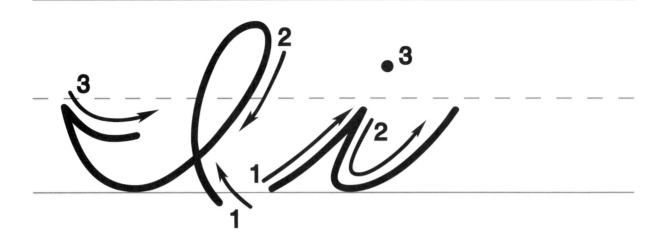

Trace with your pencil, then write.

UNITED NATIONS HEADQUARTERS

Trace with your finger.

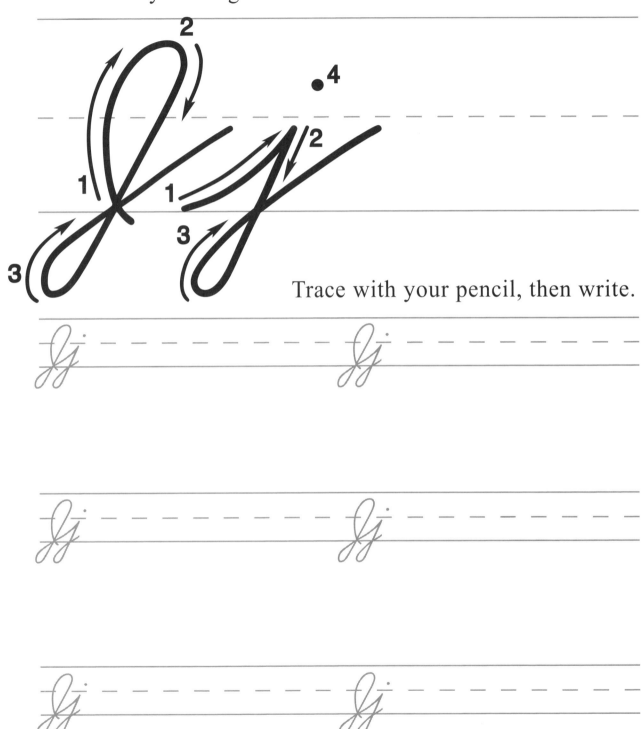

Trace with your pencil, then write.

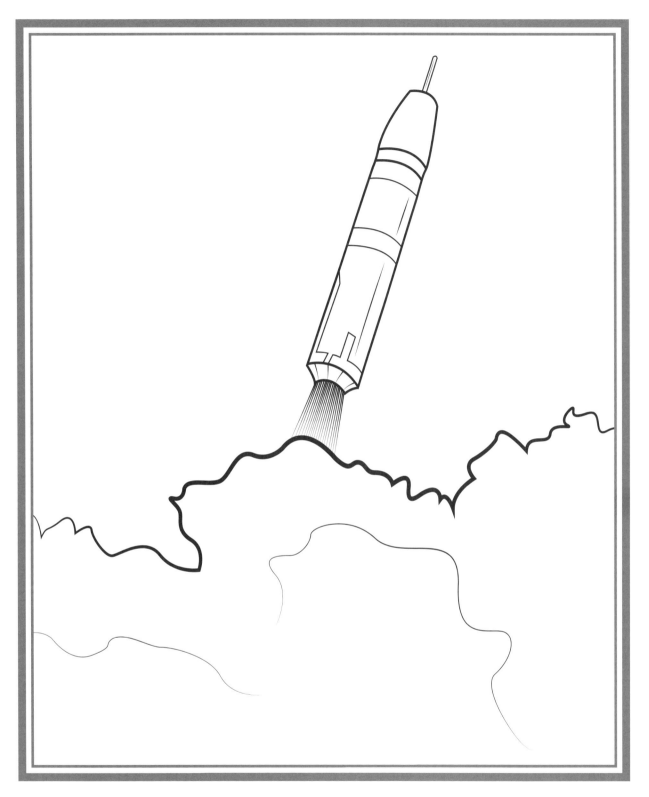

TRIDENT MISSILE

THE COLD WAR

Trace with your finger.

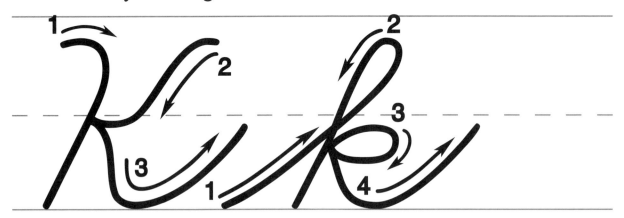

Trace with your pencil, then write.

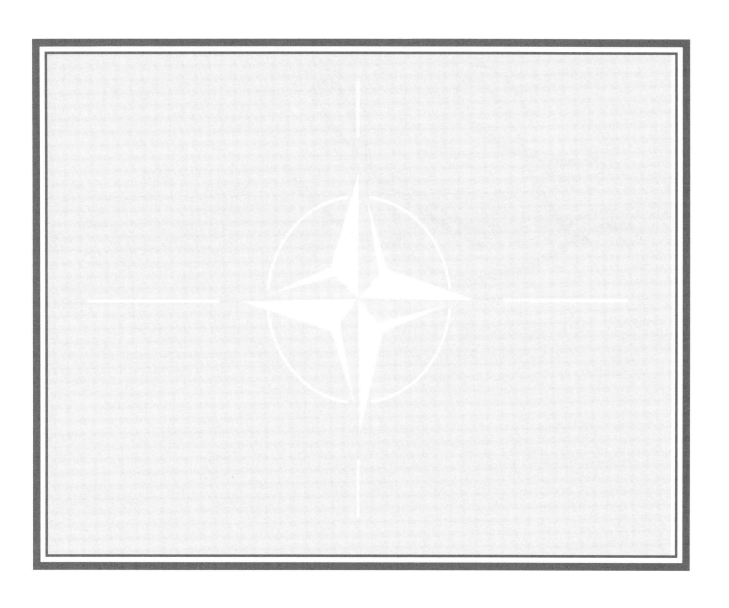

NORTH ATLANTIC TREATY ORGANIZATION (NATO) FLAG

Trace with your finger.

Trace with your pencil, then write.

THE KOREAN WAR

Trace with your finger.

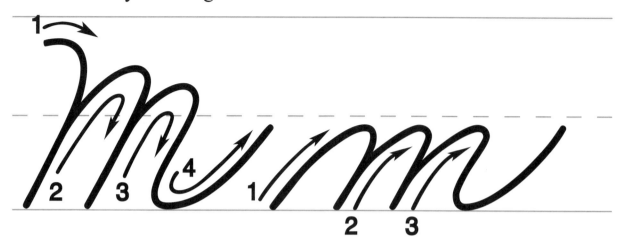

Trace with your pencil, then write.

MARTIN LUTHER KING, JR.

THE CIVIL RIGHTS MOVEMENT

Trace with your finger.

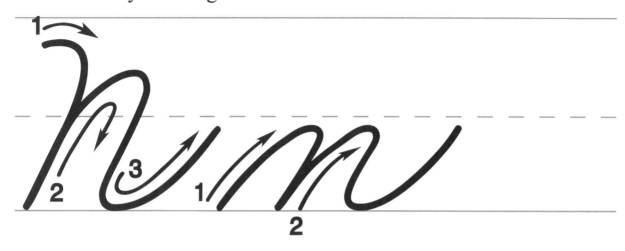

Trace with your pencil, then write.

MISSIONARIES JIM AND ELISABETH ELLIOT

Trace with your finger.

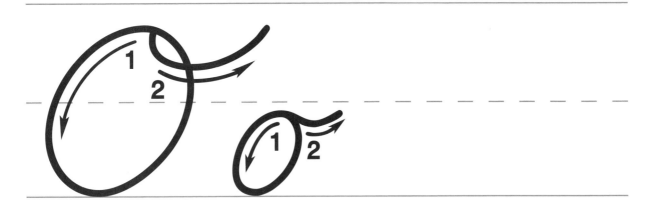

Trace with your pencil, then write.

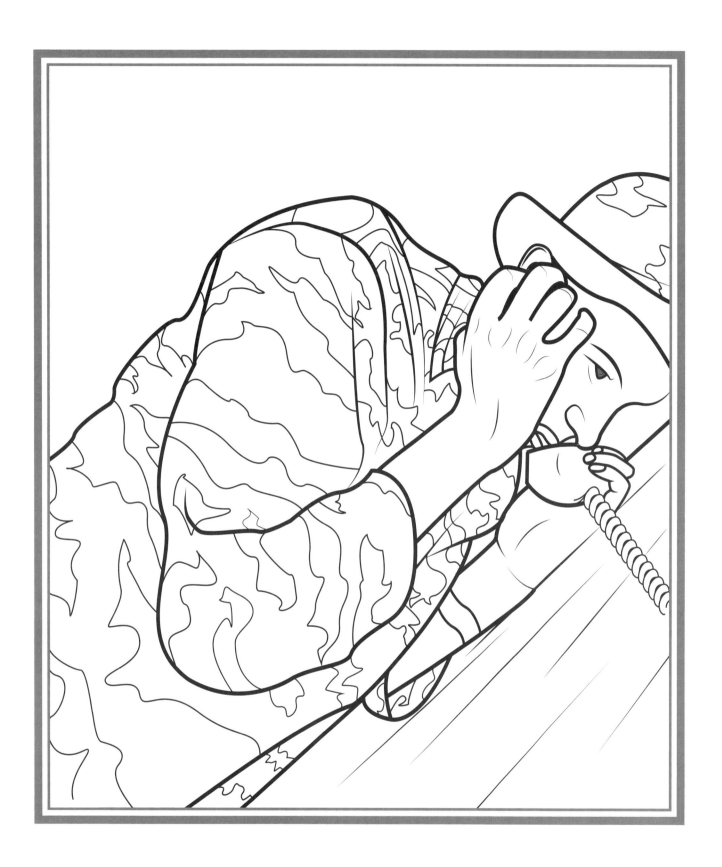

VIETNAM WAR

Trace with your finger.

Trace with your pencil, then write.

CLASSICALCONVERSATIONS.COM

U.S. Astronauts Walk on the Moon

Trace with your finger.

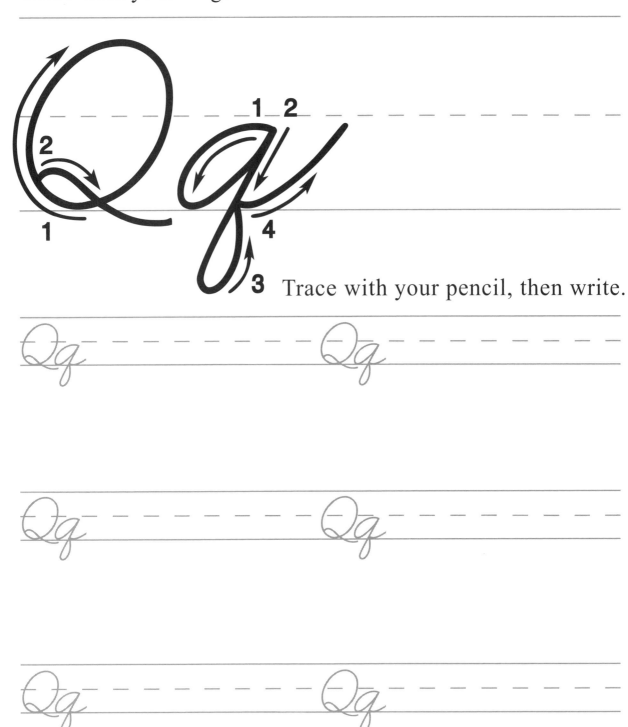

Trace with your pencil, then write.

GRAFFITI FROM THE BERLIN WALL AFTER THE FALL OF COMMUNISM IN EASTERN EUROPE

Trace with your finger.

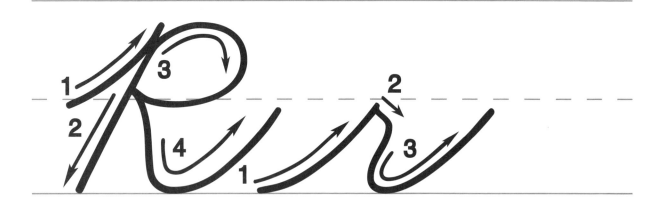

Trace with your pencil, then write.

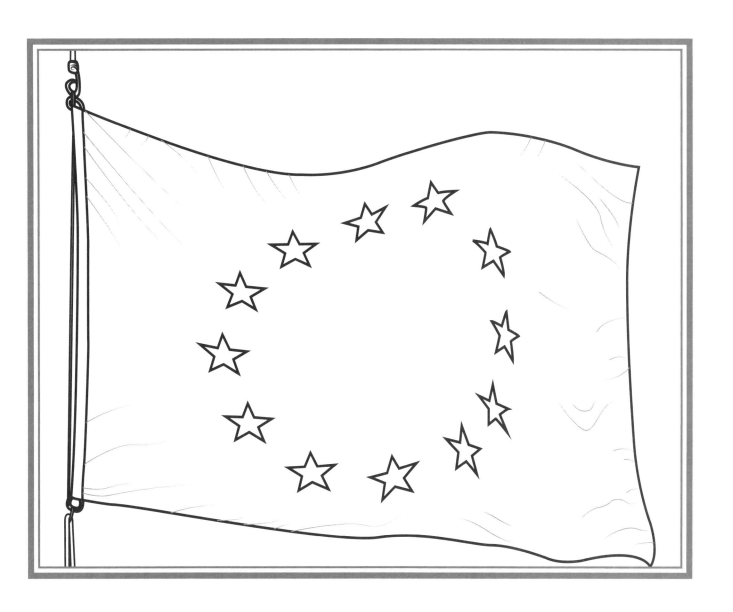

EUROPEAN UNION FLAG

Trace with your finger.

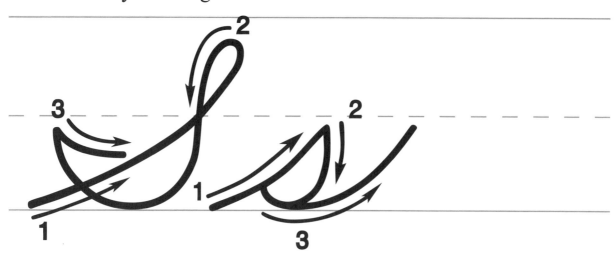

Trace with your pencil, then write.

CLASSICALCONVERSATIONS.COM

NELSON MANDELA

APARTHEID ABOLISHED IN SOUTH AFRICA

Trace with your finger.

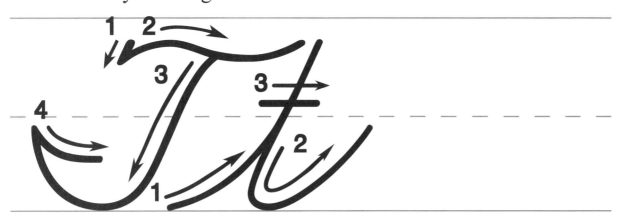

Trace with your pencil, then write.

WORLD TRADE CENTER BEFORE SEPTEMBER 11, 2001

Trace with your finger.

Trace with your pencil, then write.

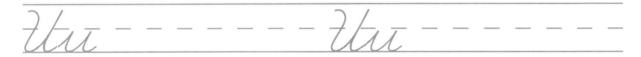

C L A S S I C A L C O N V E R S A T I O N S . C O M

SEAL OF THE PRESIDENT OF THE UNITED STATES

Trace with your finger.

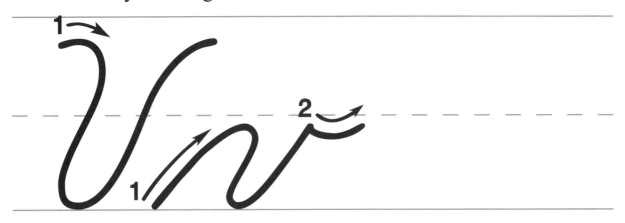

Trace with your pencil, then write.

FREE DRAWING

Trace with your finger.

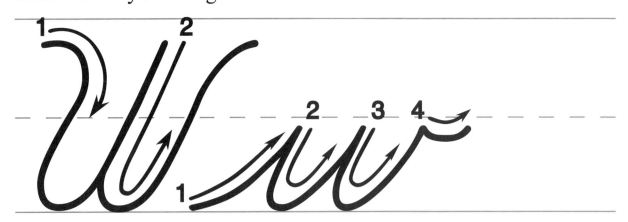

Trace with your pencil, then write.

C L A S S I C A L C O N V E R S A T I O N S . C O M

Write your name in cursive.

Trace with your finger.

Trace with your pencil, then write.

FREE DRAWING

Trace with your finger.

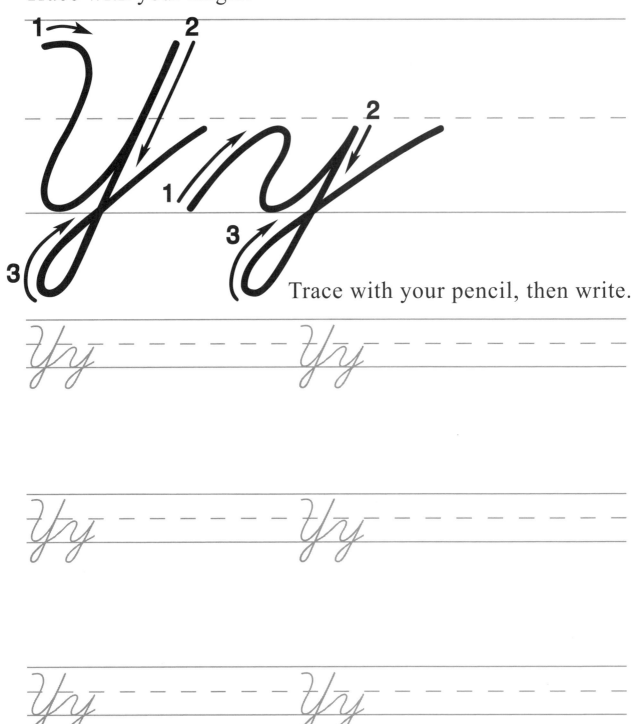

Trace with your pencil, then write.

Write your name in cursive.

Trace with your finger.

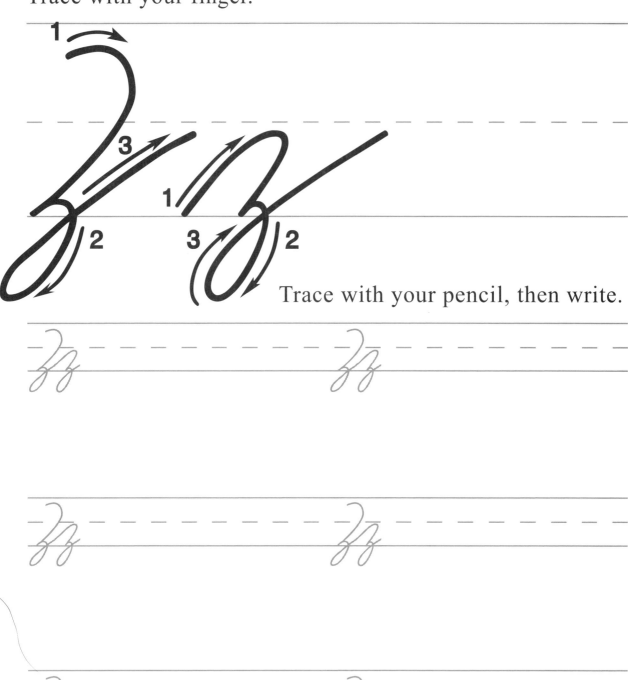

Trace with your pencil, then write.

FREE DRAWING

Image Credits

These coloring illustrations are renderings of photographs, pieces of artwork, or public domain images that represent important historical events or people from ancient to modern world history. Most drawings represent a memory peg image from Classical Conversations® MultiMedia *Classical Acts & Facts™ History Cards*. (The corresponding history card number and title is indicated in parentheses.)

Page 7 *Fowling in the Marshes* (detail), c. 1350 BC (#5 Egyptians)

Page 9 Minoan Bull-Leaper, c. 1700–1450 BC (#7 Minoans and Mycenaeans)

Page 11 Great Pyramid and Sphinx of Giza (#8 Seven Wonders of the Ancient World)

Page 13 Hanging Gardens of Babylon (#8 Seven Wonders of the Ancient World)

Page 15 Temple of Artemis (#8 Seven Wonders of the Ancient World)

Page 17 Statue of Zeus (#8 Seven Wonders of the Ancient World)

Page 19 The Mausoleum at Halicarnassus (#8 Seven Wonders of the Ancient World

Page 21 Pharos Lighthouse (#8 Seven Wonders of the Ancient World)

Page 23 Colossus of Rhodes (#8 Seven Wonders of the Ancient World)

Page 25 Pyramids of Meroë, c. 280 BC–AD 350 (#11 Kush)

Page 27 *King T'ang of Shang Dynasty*; Ma Lin, c. 1225 (#14 China's Shang Dynasty)

Page 29 Olmec Colossal Head (#6), c. 1000–600 BC (#17 Olmecs of Mesoamerica)

Page 31 Romulus and Remus (*Tiber River god,* detail), c. 2nd century AD (#25 Rome Founded by Romulus and Remus)

Page 33 Assyrian Attack by Tiglath-Pileser III, c. 730 BC (#26 Israel Falls to Assyria)

Page 35 *Confucius Presenting the Young Gautama Buddha to Lao-Tzu*, artist unknown, Qing Dynasty (#28 Lao-Tzu, Confucius, Buddha)

Page 37 *The Death of Socrates* (detail), Jacques-Louis David, 1787 (#33 Golden Age of Greece)

Page 39 Mayan Pyramid, Tulum, Mexico (#37 Mayans of Mesoamerica)

Page 41 *Hannibal Crossing the Alps*, Heinrich Leutemann, 1866 (#38 Punic Wars)

Page 43 Icon of Jesus at St. Catherine's Monastery, Mt. Sinai, 6th century AD (#55 Council of Chalcedon)

Page 45 *Mosaic of Justinian* I (detail), Basilica of San Vitale, Ravenna, c. 546 (#57 Byzantine Emperor Justinian)

Page 47 *Timbuctoo* [sic], Johann Martin Bernatz, c. 1857 (#60 Zanj and Early Ghana in Africa)

Page 49 *The Flying Carpet* (detail) Viktor Vasnetsov, 1880 (#62 Golden Age of Islam)

Page 51 *The Viking Ship*, Edward Burne-Jones, c. 1883 (#63 Vikings Raid and Trade)

Page 53 Detail of a miniature of Charlemagne being crowned emperor, *Chroniques de France ou St. Denis*, c. 14th century (#65 Charlemagne Crowned Emperor of Europe)

Page 55 Painting of Basil II (replicated from an 11th-century manuscript), artist unknown (#69 Byzantine Emperor Basil II)

Page 57 Basilica roof, Florence, Italy (#70 East-West Schism of the Church)

Page 59 Eastern-Orthodox cupola, Russia (#70 East-West Schism of the Church)

Page 61 *The Nándorfehérvár Battle*, artist unknown, 19th century (#72 The Crusades)

Page 63 Portrait of Yoritomo (copy), Fujiwara No Takanobu, 1179 (#76 Japan's Shoguns)

Page 65 *King John Signs the Magna Carta (detail)*, James W. E. Doyle, 1864 (#79 England's Magna Carta)

Page 67 *Jeanne D'Arc at the Siege of Orléans*, Jules-Eugène Lenepveu, 1890 (#82 The Hundred Years' War and Black Death)

Page 69 Drawing of a flying machine, Leonardo da Vinci, c. 1487 (#83 The Renaissance)

Page 71 *Small English Ship Dismasted in a Gale*, Willem van de Velde (II), c. 1700 (#85 Age of Exploration)

Page 73 *Ivan the Great Tearing the Khan's Letter to Pieces* (detail), Aleksey D. Kivshenko, c. 1880 (#90 Czar Ivan the Great of Russia)

Page 75 *The First Voyage* (detail), L. Prang & Co., 1893 (#92 Columbus Sails to the Caribbean)

Page 77 Imperial Crown of Austria (#93 Age of Absolute Monarchs)

Page 79 Detail from New Testament translation by Martin Luther (woodcut), c. 1522 (#94 Protestant Reformation)

Page 81 *The Whole Army Knelt in the Mud and Confessed Their Sins,* Robinson, 1909 (#95 Spanish Conquistadors in the Americas)

Page 83 *Watching the Colonists Construct James Fort*, Sidney King, c. 1957 (#100 Jamestown and Plymouth Colony Founded)

Image Credits

Page 85 Davis Vertical Feed Sewing Machine, invented 1868 (#106 Age of Industry)*

Page 87 *Washington Taking Command of the American Army Under the Old Elm at Cambridge*, Merrill, c. 1908 (#108 American Revolution and General George Washington)

Page 89 Constitution of the United States (page one), signed September 17, 1787 (#109 Madison's Constitution and the Bill of Rights)

Page 91 Map Showing Louisiana Purchase Territory (#112 Louisiana Purchase and Lewis and Clark Expedition)

Page 93 *Napoleon I on His Imperial Throne*, Jean Auguste Dominique Ingres, 1806 (#113 Napoleon Crowned Emperor of France)

Page 95 *The Star-Spangled Banner*, Percy Moran, c. 1913 (#115 The War of 1812)

Page 97 Political Map of the United States and Henry Clay (inset) (#116 The Missouri Compromise)

Page 99 Drawing of the Statue of Liberty (detail), Kelly Steigerwald (#117 Immigrants Flock to America)

Page 101 *The Monroe Doctrine, 1823* (detail), Allyn Cox, 1973 (#118 The Monroe Doctrine)

Page 103 *End of the Trail* (bronze), James Earle Fraser, 1929 (#120 Cherokee Trail of Tears)

Page 105 Drawing of panning for gold, Kelly Steigerwald (# 121 U.S. Westward Expansion)

Page 107 *The United States Senate, A.D. 1850* (detail), P.F. Rothermel, c. 1855 (#123 The Compromise of 1850 and the *Dred Scott* Decision)

Page 109 Steam Locomotive (#106 Age of Industry)

Page 111 Allan Pinkerton, President Lincoln, and Major General John A. McClernand at Antietam, MD, Alexander Gardner, October 3, 1862 (#127 Lincoln's War Between the States)

Page 113 Ulysses S. Grant, 1869–1877 (#166 Johnson, Grant, Hayes, Garfield)

Page 115 *The Charge of the Rough Riders* (detail), Frederic Remington, 1898 (#132 The Spanish-American War)

Page 117 Belgian policeman and French policeman, World War I Document Archive (#136 World War I and President Wilson)

Page 119 Drawing of *Starry Night* by Vincent van Gogh, Kelly Steigerwald (#139 Modern Period of the Arts)

Page 121 *Migrant Mother*, Dorothea Lange, 1936 (#140 The Great Depression and the New Deal)

Page 123 USS *Bunker Hill* at Okinawa, Tony Faccone, Archival Research Catalog, U.S. National Archives (#141 World War II and President Franklin D. Roosevelt)

Page 125 Josef Stalin, Library of Congress, LC-USW33-019081-C (#142 Stalin of the USSR and the Katyn Massacre)

Page 127 United Nations Headquarters, Jeremy Edwards (#143 The United Nations Formed)

Page 129 First launch of a Trident missile, 1977 (#144 The Cold War)

Page 131 Drawing of the flag of NATO, Kelly Steigerwald (#148 North Atlantic Treaty Organization)

Page 133 Korean girl carrying brother in Haengju, Korea, Air Force Major R. V. Spencer, 1951 (#149 The Korean War)

Page 135 Dr. Martin Luther King, Jr., Dick DeMarsico, 1964 (#150 Martin Luther King, Jr. and the Civil Rights Movement)

Page 137 *Elisabeth and Jim Elliot*, Ralph Grady James, 2011 (#151 Jim and Elisabeth Elliot, Missionaries to Ecuador)

Page 139 Soldier firing M-16 while another calls for support, Company D, 151st (Ranger) Infantry, 1969 (#153 The Vietnam War)

Page 141 Edwin "Buzz" Aldrin and the US flag on the moon, Neil A. Armstrong, July 20, 1969 (#154 U.S. Astronauts Walk on the Moon)

Page 143 Graffiti from the Berlin Wall, Action Press (#157 Fall of Communism in Eastern Europe)

Page 145 Drawing of the European Union flag, Kelly Steigerwald (#158 European Union Formed)

Page 147 Nelson Mandela in Johannesburg, Gauteng *South Africa The Good News*, 13 May 1998 (#159 Apartheid Abolished in South Africa)

Page 149 Drawing of the World Trade Center before September 11, 2001, Kelly Steigerwald (#160 September 11, 2001)

Page 151 Drawing of the Seal of the President of the United States, Kelly Steigerwald (U.S. Presidents Cards)

*The sewing machine represents the age of industry as a time when intricate machines made large-scale production of products possible. The sewing machine represented in the drawing was invented later, but it is representative of machines used during the time period of the age of industry.

Have you ever thought about homeschooling?

You're not alone. There are an estimated *2 million* homeschooled children in the United States. Why are so many parents making this choice? A recent poll of families in Classical Conversations yielded ten reasons to choose homeschooling:

1. Religious reasons
2. Positive socialization
3. Academic quality
4. School/state separation
5. Family relationships
6. Custom-made education plans
7. Efficiency
8. Emphasis on mastery, not grades
9. Safety
10. Low cost

Have you resisted the idea
because you don't think you can do it on your own?

Classical Conversations offers the support of a community near you. Families with students ages pre-K to 12th grade gather one day a week to study together. Trained parents serve as tutors to lead you and your children through oral presentations, science experiments, and fine arts projects. Families in the Foundations program (K4 through sixth grade) study math, science, history, Latin and English grammar, and geography through fun songs and interactive games.

Families have chosen our communities because:

- We've been meeting together since 1997.
- Our directors and tutors receive over forty hours of training each year.
- Even four-year-olds make weekly presentations to their classes.
- Our youngest students complete weekly science experiments and fine arts projects—no mess at home!
- Experienced parents are available each week to mentor you.
- Students (and parents!) have found their best friends here.
- Communities offer supplemental services such as standardized testing, transcripts, and parent webinars about college preparation.
- Parents receive three days of FREE training each summer.
- Meeting with a trained tutor once a week helps families continue to homeschool through middle school and high school.
- We offer comprehensive online resources and tools to support and equip you on your personal homeschool journey.
- Our communities offer a weekly support network so that you can homeschool *for* yourself, but not *by* yourself.

Learn more by attending a local Classical Conversations Information Meeting or visit a Classical Conversations community Open House. Visit our website's Event Calendar today to find a community and events near you.

Additional products from

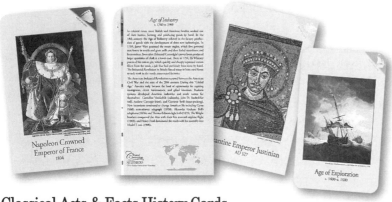

Classical Acts & Facts History Cards

Classical Conversations has developed its own timeline of 161 historical events, representing major cultures on every continent. The events are divided into seven ages and produced as cards similar to our Classical Acts & Facts Science Cards, with the event title on the front and a fuller description of the event on the back. Each card front also contains a beautiful memory peg image. Images were chosen to serve families all the way through cultural studies in the upper levels of Challenge. The back of each card also includes a world map, pinpointing the event location, and a general timeline, illustrating when the event occurred relative to known history.

Classical Christian Education Made Approachable

Have you heard about classical, Christian education but don't know what those words mean? Are you intimidated by the prospect of giving your children an education so different from your own? Let this booklet answer your questions. Discover the tools of learning that can lead your family from knowledge to understanding to wisdom.